Little Footprints On Her Heart

June Roshni Lobo

BookLeaf Publishing

Presentation by *BookLeaf Publishing*

Web: www.bookleafpub.com

E-mail: info@bookleafpub.com

ISBN: 9789357218498

First edition 2023

DEDICATION

- For my Mom and dad; Laura & Anthony who always taught me how to pray innocently like a child and never lose my faith no matter what.

- For my Mother in law, Joanet whose faith is wildly amazing and has been my strongest companion on sunny and cloudy days.

- For my Husband, Sunil - I will always love you!

- For my sister-in-law Sidd and the apple of her eye and my godchild, Rhea.

- Last but not the least - For Savannah, the heartbeat in my womb.

ACKNOWLEDGEMENT

I wish to extend my gratitude to the women who have significantly contributed by sharing their first-hand experiences with me in order to narrate these poems on their behalf, as untold stories of their unborn joys, or in the form of prayers and petitions made for offspring.
Not all women can express although people believe that women are better at showing emotions than men.
I am deeply touched by the husbands of such women who have articulated what their wives went through or have experienced through their miscarriage or journey of losing their little ones.
I would also like to thank my husband Sunil for being my loyal critic and although his detailed criticism gets us riled up, it has ironically turned me into a much stronger woman and made me wiser in thought, word, and deed.
It is simply a blessing to be surrounded by people who care for you and advise you for the better, so that you are taken care of, and so that you do the right thing, and I cannot thank my family and in-laws, enough for being my spine. Through thick and thin, we've been in it together!

A special note of gratitude to Sr. Conchita and Sr. Lovely who taught me to pray and never give up.

A big thank you to my mother and mother-in-law for always planting healthy seeds of faith in me and always praying for me.

Last but not the least, I thank my darling dad who was my best friend and always encouraged me to move on but stay strong in prayer because "ask and you shall receive." he said.

PREFACE

The one thing I wanted to see in life, was the smiling face of my baby cradled in my palms; and when I realized that not everyone gets what they want, as a woman I walked through many roads of desperation, despair, desire, and delirium.
It took me a while and; various elements kept me afloat through that journey.
Trying to have a baby by going through the drill of prescriptions, needles, and pills and then accepting my fate gracefully, was a journey in itself.

Speaking to friends who have had the same experience and understanding their state of mind and relating to them, based on my own stories, led me to pen down words that I have stitched together to make, "Little footprints on her Heart." - The little steps that were left as prints on the heart of the mother when the baby left her womb, unannounced.

Although my dream attempted to make its way to me, it stayed briefly in my womb, allowing me to make conversation with that heartbeat I saw after 3 months of being pregnant. I wanted

to celebrate and tell all and sundry that I was going to be a mother!
It was a week post my declaration that I went for my follow-up appointment and I was told that we lost the heartbeat.
All I witnessed was a little movement on that screen which was my baby's heart beating. My anticipation and happiness died down when the heartbeat slowly vanished away leaving a vacuum inside me.
I had no idea what I did or how it happened. If only one could go in there and search and call out to it. But I hadn't even told what I wished to name her.

"Courtesy demands, you seek permission to leave!" I thought.
I would've taught her that when she came into my world!
How impatient was she to just tiptoe away from me, just leaving her footprints engraved on the walls of my heart?

Having said that, the bitter experience also made me a stronger person, allowing me to look back after a while and laugh at my misery because come on! Life is much more than just having a child, taking accountability and responsibility till he or she turns 18 or 21, and spending sleepless nights changing diapers and singing lullabies. Maybe my path was different. I knew within my bone I was maternal however I could always channel that energy elsewhere by doing good to society, being charitable, funding an orphan, or even educating a child who needed it. It all slowly unraveled itself to me and today I could proudly say, I am what I am.

I may not have it all, but I am so content with the other blessings I have.

The Prayer

On bent knees, I shed a tear
The sun shone down on me but I still cried
It's been so long and yet unclear
Along with my tears, even the flowers I offered, have died.

Is this a test or just the worst nightmare?
In the distance, I see mothers with their happy little ones.
Am I to wait longer, or does anyone up there care?
my patience is tried and my stomach bitterly just churns.

Bless me with that one... Just one glorious gift today.
my hands I lift in utmost desperation
look at me before you consider turning me away.
I see raised eyebrows who are now calling me "barren".

My promise remains that I will fulfil as a mother.
I will nurture, nourish and create a path of goodness

Answer this one prayer and I will bother you no further.
I know I am worthy of your abundant grace in all fairness!

Your Return To The Big Blue Window

The image of your heart beating was blurred yet very true.
I was only joyful because I finally was a part of the race.
Were you not content with the surroundings you were put into?
Was it just wrong timing, an unknown world, and not the right place?

The only desire I had was for your eyes to meet mine.
I knew you watched me quietly from that big blue window.
He took my hand and said, It's most certainly going to be fine.
After all, it was just us, and probably you who understood this woe.

I practiced lines to say to you whenever you arrived home.
Even the family waited in anticipation of your glorious arrival.
My soul says you knew I was right here with arms so warm.

Then why did that affirming assurance turn into
cold betrayal?

Were you mine? I sometimes wonder in bitter
agony.
I imagine you, still looking at me from that big
blue window.
It's a cold cage of reality and somewhere it
teases my vulnerability
But you will someday step away from there and
hold my hand; this I know.

She Left Without a Word

In moments of desperation, I searched for her face.
In a dream, she was tucked away and asleep in my heart.
I wondered at times how I'd feel in her gentle embrace.
The feeling of being a mother was an emotion that sparked.

In keeping her alive, I may not have been successful,
her heartbeat on that screen; still so vivid in my mind.
It was a moment of joy and tears that made life so blissful.
and then that heartbeat vanished and life was just unkind!

Wasn't my womb warm enough to keep her cozy and safe?
I felt unworthy and questions filled my troubled head,
She just left. I imagined her in an unknown world, like a waif.
For now, I parked my tears aside, but my desire wasn't dead.

It's her..

"Let me go, my Mumma's waiting," I
pictured her crying in another world.
"Not now, as it's not yet time," they said and
held her hand.
As you can see; my wild wait led me to vivid
imaginations that swirled.
It was a torment, I wasn't willing to bear, cry
over, or even stand.

I always thought it was "her"; within my heart, I
created a bond.
I even named her and addressed her in prayer
and a dream.
If only I could have a glimpse of her face, by
using a magic wand.
At least the hope I had through all this, began to
slightly gleam.

She would arrive someday in my life; that was
the hope.
I was reminded of the faith of the childless
mother; "Hannah".
somewhere my faith said, there was a way, and
yes there was scope.
This made me even establish a name; - "we shall
call her, Savannah!"

I Put Her To Bed

when I came of an age where my conscience
said, it was time.
As a growing girl, I envisioned a home, my man,
and beautiful sunny days.
My dreams and fantasies in my head were like a
chime.
But a girl with so many expectations must also
be ready for God's ways.

I'll hold my child in my arms, I thought, and sing
her a lullaby.
She'll learn to crawl, walk, talk, and one day
even run.
Dreams don't always come true and some
gradually putrefy.
Reality is always something else other than the
stories one has spun.

But it's really all right, every time I'd convince
myself.
Being a mother is not the biggest goal one has to
achieve.
so I put my dream to bed or maybe even
book-ended it on a shelf.
There are other blessings in many other forms;
This I do believe.

For The Time They Had Her

She made a mother's wish, as she held her little finger.
She said, "be my angel forever and I shall always be your friend.
May no harm ever come to you, and let your dreams be bigger.
I shall be your companion and confidante till the very end."

As she grew up, she was a sports enthusiast and a drummer rockstar.
That's at least what her doting father said when he fondly remembered her
"The time spent with her was a story of a lifetime. We're content with that. We are."
he'd say it in mere assurance; to avoid her memory from going into a blur.

A day hasn't gone by that she hasn't been missed.
In their thoughts and their minds, in their souls, she will always be.
Yes, they cried and laid white lilies on the stone they kissed.
"Reunite us again soon," they said with faith,
"This is our humble plea."

The "Well wishers"

"Try from the top; don't move and stay at the
bottom."
"Get adventurous," they said, "to your side and
then to his side."
Positions and techniques were shared by all;
like, to a pilot, in a Notum.
My anxiety, and oh! even the loss of libido now,
were in a tide.

Slowly and steadily, the pain evolved into
something humorous.
And then I started wondering, "Am I cut out to
be a mother?"
The needles blotched my skin and they made no
difference to my uterus.
By now, I desperately craved a drink as much as
I'd sacrificed it, I gather.

Days and months passed by, post the uterus and
fertility battle.
The tears were dried and I now reached for my
eyeliner and mascara
enough of these bitter tonics; both by doctors
and by people who tattle
I decided to move on, have fun and end this
agonizing era!

The "Womb-versation"

"I cannot wait to see you," I said and touched
my baby bump.
On the monitor, they showed me her tiny beating
existence.
I had to waddle with caution but in reality, I
wanted to jump!
Although she was already inside me, I still felt
the distance.

To all and sundry we thought we'd announce this
happy news
An evening of friends, relatives, and family in
celebration.
Our hearts said it was a girl and a name we had
to wisely choose
My heart was as joyous and vibrant as the bright
decoration.

We conversed with the bump and blessed it
every time.
Each day I'd wonder if she listened to our voices
inside.
The feeling of carrying her was eternal and just
sublime
I said, "I love you little one." I dint hear it, but I
know she replied.

Grievance vs the Gift of Grace

She was a daughter and she was taught it all
Her mother corrected her mistakes, resulting in a lesson.
Her father reprimanded her but hugged her when she'd bawl.
First teachers, they were; and to them, she was a treasured possession.

She grew up one day and became a wonderful wife
Loving she was, caring, committed, and loyal
She had in her savings, all their teachings and advice on life
Strong yet humble, obedient yet equal, this she knew was crucial

The time had come when she desired to be a mother
Would this also be a role she'd fulfill to the fullest?
There was nothing on earth she wanted more, one way or the other
The never coming stork led her to do her bit and best.

"A child I will bear," she said with agonizing anticipation.
She was haunted by dark doubt and deadly disability.
their consistent attempts to fix the challenge led to her aggression
"I will receive this grace!" she stated with faith and avidity.

On That Bench In Church.

After what feels like a lifetime of mere struggle,
I sit on that bench staring at his closed eyes.
Today it all feels like it was a desire in a bubble
Was it just his ways or a blessing in disguise?

A woman kneeling in front of him is with child
I sit on that bench staring at his closed eyes
The pain, the agony, the emptiness are alive and
it has just piled
Was it just his ways or a blessing in disguise?

Someone celebrates the happiness of offspring
I sit on that bench staring at his closed eyes.
The wait makes me swallow hard and my eyes
begin to sting
Was it just his ways or a blessing in disguise?

"Where is your baby?", this question; a
cane-whacking torment.
I still sit on that bench staring at his closed eyes.
I pushed that ball of grief down my throat; my
emotions were just dormant.
Was it just his ways or a blessing in disguise?

I'm at an age today where I may have achieved it all
His arms are wide open on that cross but closed are his eyes.
Blessings still come my way and maybe motherhood isn't a call
But I know he hears me because on that bench I left my cries.

Curiosity Vs Fertility

"So, when's the Good news?" They asked me
with curiosity.
Talk about the interest they expressed in my life!
"In his time, I guess," I said with susceptibility.
The process of even conceiving was mere pain
and strife!

"It's been almost a decade, and yet no
offspring?" questioned another.
It all led to more pressure, embarrassment and so
much confusion.
Oh, the agony of this blessed society, if you're
not a mother!
Who knew the plight I went through with every
pill, prick, and sex position?

"Stay tuned!" I'd say every month with a wink of
humour.
Hiding away my anxiety, now came so naturally
to me.
Each time I'd get closer to the date I'd think I
was getting warmer.
But alas! that red line on the stick just made me
exclaim, "just, let me be!"

The Haunting Faces

The images of babies once left me elated.
I always wanted one, I could someday call my own.
but when it was time, the "process" left me frustrated.
I still patiently waited but the stork had somehow flown.

I saw it happen for friends, associates, and family.
What on earth was taking so long on this side?
I'd congratulate them with joy but asked God endlessly.
I expressed a happy being of myself to all, but I lied.

Slowly with time, those images of babies teased me
I'd look at them and quickly scroll away. God knows why
I realized; that a part of that joy, I may never be.
My wait had taken so long and still, time was flying by.

A letter To My Uterus

I decided to write to her one day and so I began
"My dear Uterus, you're going through so much;
I must admit.
Consider this, my apology, and forgive me as
soon as you can.
It's just a phase and you must know we just need
not quit.

Their intrusions in your little space will be
normal
your roof needs fixing and maybe somewhere
your floor.
I thought I must warn you before you and I get
into a quarrel.
it's just something you and I in this situation
cannot ignore.

I write to you so that like me you too are
prepared
We need to make this place a liveable little home
for her.
There's so much happening, I confess. I too am
scared.
I'm seeking your cooperation, yours truly, an
aspiring mother."

The Unwarranted For Banter

"When's the good news?" Curiously, they asked me.
"The price of onions is at its lowest!" I exclaimed.
With glorious sarcasm, I smiled back gracefully.
In my mind, my middle finger stood up unashamed.

They blinked back in bewilderment and dropped their jaws.
"She doesn't seem to understand." they pointed out.
"An age for childbearing, she must consider, before menopause."
I knew the battle I was battling but chose to leave them in doubt.

Pieces of advice on "baby-making" came like sweets on a festive day.
I listened with an acknowledging warm "nod" and "yes".
The banter exited and I'd reach for wine and my crystal ashtray.
One way to respond was to keep it within and act with grace!

Road Trip To The Clinic

"How many times in a week do you try?" she asked.
Her face was as stoic as a soldier's sturdy face.
"We do it as often as can", I responded, unmasked.
Our conversation was more like "cutting to the chase."

Visiting the Gynaecologist, for me now was a horrid ritual.
It was funny how many times I had to spread my legs!
From white satin sheets to cold cotton ones, became habitual.
an ordeal of monitoring seeds, the clock, the dates, and my eggs!

Who said, it wasn't fun? we also called it an adventure.
Now, one had to be positive through anxiety and anticipation.
A "blue movie" with approved characters and unwanted censure.
which the clinic and "crew" enjoyed while I lay there in abomination.

The curious "Catty" Mother in Law.

I chose not to eat and sat aside from the table.
"Are you pregnant?" she asked, with eyes so bright.
I rolled my eyes in a way; she probably thought I'm unstable.
she watched me closely like I was that red cloth in a bullfight.

When we drank together one evening, I extended my empty glass.
"Pour me some wine darling," I said to my husband standing by
She suddenly showed me her eyes signalling to make it a pass.
Irritated by this constant monitoring, I now needed to get high!

To see my offspring was her desire more than mine
honestly, some things just take time; how does one explain?
but her dream and my infertility pushed me to draw the line.

"I must do something," I thought before she asks me again.

I counted my fertile days on my fingers one late evening,
"Are you pregnant?" she asked, "Are you doing it right?"
I smiled back in response but inside, at her, I was screaming.
"We're still working on it," I said politely, "you can come watch tonight!"

I Learned..

An emotion so deep, it still stays stuck like a
leech.
Even if I tried it never left the chambers of my
heart
Would I just let go of the feeling; or what limit
would I reach?
She left my womb, but her brief existence would
never break apart.

I made my peace with the ways of nature now
what more could I do? How much more could I
try?
There were no more answers to why, what,
when, and how.
She may return but today, she watches me from
the sky.

I have no more tears to shed, and I guess I've
moved on
Life means much more than being just parked at
one low.
I learned the art of being content, and prayers, I
banked upon.
It wasn't easy at first, but time taught me to be
content; this I know.

Count Your Blessings.

I had a dream as I walked through the phases of life.
My mother's lessons were imbibed within my soul.
"With blue skies", she said, "come rain, pain, and strife.
but, making it sunny on cloudy days should always be your goal."

"I'd have a home, a man to love, and children I'd call my own.
I imagined how life would dish out to me its true blessings.
"I'd treat every day like a new dawned glorious morn."
even if the tide of time turns and some moments are pressing.

With time I realized my one dream kept fading away.
I had the house, and my adorable man, but a silent white world.
I still counted every blessing and agreed for the desire to go astray.
"You don't get everything," said mom. "That's just life, My girl."

The Choice To Move On

It's been a while now and maybe I've forgotten
There was a time when I just went all berserk.
I parked the grief somewhere and the saner I've
gotten.
all that drama and procedure was just ugly work

So now it's just me, the big house, and my man.
The room I had prepared for her still has the
cradle
There were pills and prescriptions in place of my
beer can
Managing to survive the storm, was indeed
commendable!

I was once haunted by the gynaecologist and
laboratory.
Now I am at peace as I have those ghosts
blocked
The series I went through would've made a
marvellous story,
The decision was to stay happy and have some
desires locked!

I'm Ending It!

Yes, it's been a while, and no there's no baby yet
I'm still a happy being and you can't see that I bet.
I gave it my best and tried everything that was right.
A dark cloudy season now sees the sun out and bright!

You think I am shallow but there's nothing I can do now
I'm mute on my scene. I'm done with the drama and I'm taking a bow.
Please don't ask me what's happening. Oh, come on you better stop!
because when it happens, to all, I'll announce, from the mountaintop!

…And Then Dad Said..

I witnessed a brand new day and on me, the sun
shone.
It felt like I'd fought a war and now was the time
to rest.
I made a promise never to cry and I'd write that
in stone.
It did become challenging at first but I knew I'd
given it my best.

Dad said, "Not everyone gets what they want in
life."
He knew my eyes better than words could
explain.
How right he was, and I worked toward getting
out of my strife.
I stepped out of the gloom and kissed goodbye
to the pain.

"Maybe you've tried everything," dad said, "and
you're moving on.
But don't forget, he remembers your tears and
your long lament.
Keep asking like a child and don't ever consider
your prayers gone.

He will one day give you more than you need, without your consent."

So my plea to all those women out there is to wait.
Don't quit or give up and stay strong in your motherhood.
Childbearing alone does not determine your future or fate.
whatever happens- happens for the best and your good!